CW00429991

 *project*

COLOSSIANS

Written by **Anne Pangbourne**
and **Brian Parfitt**

Design by **Catherine Jackson**

Published by CPAS
Adult Training & Resources Unit
Athena Drive
Tachbrook Park
WARWICK
CV34 6NG
Tel: (01926) 334242

ISBN 1 8976 6019 7

Church Pastoral Aid Society
Registered Charity No 1007820
A company limited by guarantee

Choosing to be Free

'His letters contain some things that are hard to understand' (2 Peter 3:16)! If a fellow New Testament author had problems with Paul's epistles, it is hardly surprising that sometimes we need a little help too. This addition to the Project series aims to help groups understand Paul's letter to the Colossians. Each study offers an explanation of the selected passage to share with the group. Clear undersanding will provide a sound basis for discussing the relevance of Colossians for us today.

Each section also contains an alternative study method. These use a variety of approaches, some of which you may have come across before, some of which may be new. As well as being useful for the passages in Colossians, they should also prove to be useful tools for further exploration of other parts of the Bible.

Alongside them are the usual features of this Project series, such as ideas for worship and prayer and Sunday Extra to help you link house group studies with the Sunday teaching programme. We hope that this book will help churches make challenging discoveries in a letter which contains vital lessons for today.

Contents

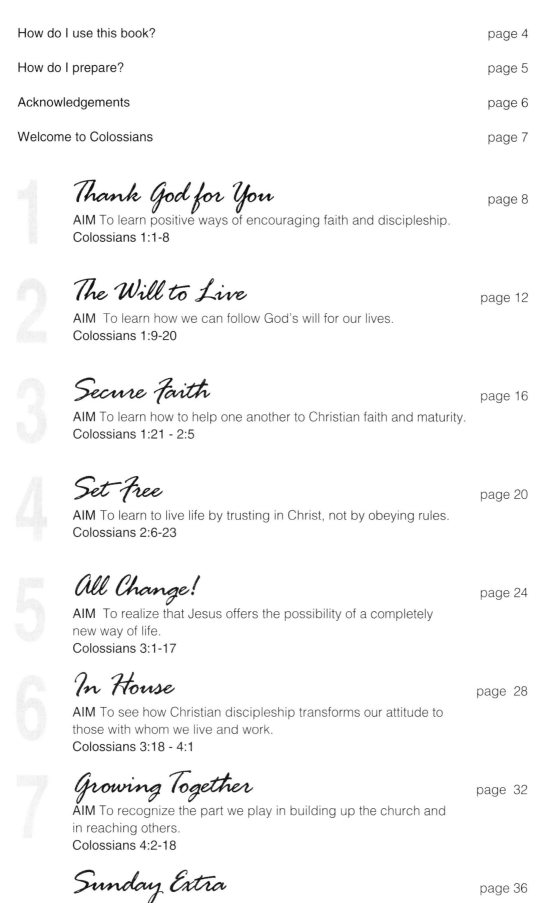

How do I Use This Book?

Project Colossians contains seven studies. Each of them is a complete unit, but they also follow on from one another. Within each study you will find the following:

ON THE FIRST TWO PAGES are the GROUP SHEETS. These may be photocopied so that all the members of the group can see them. This is an exception to the copyright. *(Please see details in copyright note on the title page.)* Each GROUP SHEET has all the basic material for a Bible study on the week's passage and contains...

 AIM The main point which should emerge from that week's study.

 BEGIN HERE Discussion starters, often of a general nature, helping people to share their own experience and to begin to think about the topic.

 BIBLE STUDY This begins with:

 Introduction An explanation of the passage as a whole which can be read by, or to, the group. References to the questions which follow are given. You can either discuss the questions after each section of the notes, or leave them until you have read all the notes.

 Questions These help the group explore the meaning and message of the passage.

 ACTION Steps to take to apply what has been learned in a practical way.

ON THE THIRD AND FOURTH PAGES, for easy reference by the group leader, are:

 ALTERNATIVE METHOD OF STUDY This gives you another way of looking at the Bible passage and could be used before discussing the questions in the BIBLE STUDY.

 ADDITIONAL QUESTIONS These provide another set of questions. You can use some of them as alternatives to the questions on the GROUP SHEETS — or they could all be used as an alternative Bible study to the one on the GROUP SHEET.

 BIBLE NOTES Explanation of individual verses to give you a fuller understanding of the passage. You may like to read some of them to the group when you think it might be helpful.

 WORSHIP & PRAYER Ideas to help the group worship and pray together. Suitable hymns and songs are listed in the Sunday Extra pages at the back of the book.

AT THE BACK OF THE BOOK on pages 36 to 39 you will find

 SUNDAY EXTRA Ideas for adapting the theme for Sunday Worship either before or after the group meetings. Hymns and songs for use on Sunday or during the meeting are listed here. The songs are taken from Mission Praise (Combined Edition).

How Do I Prepare?

1 PREPARE YOURSELF

Pray about the passage, the study, the group and yourself as leader.

Work quickly through the GROUP SHEETS, as if you were an ordinary group member. Jot down notes, questions, and areas to expand or work on. Be honest with yourself and let God teach you as you prepare.

Again read through the passage and the notes. Be guided by the AIM.

2 PLAN YOUR APPROACH

Decide how you are going to tackle the study. There are a number of possible approaches to each passage. You may decide to take two weeks over a study in order to make use of all the material.

The Bible study on the GROUP SHEETS has a helpful explanation of the passage. This can be read aloud to the group or read in silence by the members. The questions which follow are about the way the passage applies to us today. Decide on your approach: you can leave the questions until you have read all the introduction, or you can discuss each question at the point marked in the notes.

You can use the material on the GROUP SHEETS every week. Or, on the principle that 'variety is the spice of life', you can use the ALTERNATIVE METHOD OF STUDY for some of your meetings. This will give you another 'way in' to what the passage says and it can be used in place of the explanation of the passage on the GROUP SHEETS. (Each ALTERNATIVE METHOD offers a different approach; these can be used for looking at other passages in future meetings.) You can also use the ADDITIONAL QUESTIONS to substitute for, or supplement, the questions on the GROUP SHEETS. Make sure you always include BEGIN HERE and ACTION.

3 ASSESS THE TIMING

You will not have time to cover all the material so don't set out thinking this is the aim. Marks will not be deducted if the paper is not completed! You need to use what is appropriate and helpful to your group. Think carefully about the timing of each section. We have not put down suggestions for times, since each group will have different priorities. However we suggest that, as you prepare, you write down your target time for each section.

Try to keep to a basic framework each week and allocate times for prayer, reading, discussion and coffee, even though you may feel a longer prayer time, for example, is appropriate on some occasions. It is good to end promptly so that those who need to do so can go, leaving others to chat if they wish.

Acknowledgements

We are particularly grateful to Anne Pangbourne who originally produced these studies on Colossians for the house groups at Christ Church, Ore, and has since reworked her material for this Project series. We are also grateful to Janet Parfitt who has re-typed it all, to Rory Keegan, who has helped edit it and Catherine Jackson, who has done all the design work. Colossians shows us Christians working as a team to build up the church, with each one playing their part. Project Colossians has depended on a team too!

Welcome to Colossians

WHO WERE THE COLOSSIANS?

As far as we know Paul never visited the church at Colossae. It is believed that the church was founded by a man named Epaphras, who had probably heard Paul preaching in Ephesus. When Paul wrote this letter, and the letter to Philemon, it appears that Epaphras was imprisoned with him (Philemon 23; Colossians 4:12). The church at Colossae probably met in homes, certainly Philemon was a Christian at Colossae and had a group meeting in his house (Philemon 2).

WHY WAS PAUL WRITING TO THEM?

The Church was under attack from false teaching, which undermined the basics of the Christian faith:

The Lordship of Jesus Christ — the creator and Lord of the universe who became man, who died, rose again and ascended to heaven where he resumed his supreme place at the right hand of God, from which he will come to judge mankind.

Freedom from the Law — so that we do not have to earn our salvation by following a set of rules. Instead Christ by his death forgave our sin and took away the barrier between God and humanity, which was caused by our failure to keep the Law.

Resurrection Life — by his resurrection Jesus triumphed over the power of sin and death, and through the coming of the Holy Spirit gives us strength both to live as he did, and to bring others to a knowledge of his gift of eternal life.

WHAT IS THE LETTER ABOUT?

In the letter Paul reaffirms both the supreme place of Christ over all things and the freedom he brings from the Law. He goes on to outline the shape which a life of Christian discipleship should take. Colossians clearly proclaims basic Christian faith and teaching. It gives us a challenging insight into what is required of those who choose to follow Jesus.

WHAT CAN WE LEARN FROM IT?

Under the influence of New Age thinking and the pressure to be a multi-cultural, multi-faith society, the modern vogue is for a 'mix and match' religion. In contrast, Colossians challenges us about the supreme place Christ should have in our beliefs — and about the way our allegiance to him should shape our lives. In the Decade of Evangelism, Colossians teaches us again the essentials of our faith, it strengthens our understanding and equips us to go out and make disciples, ready and prepared 'to give an answer to everyone who asks ... the reason for the hope that you have'(1 Peter 3:15).

Group Sheet **1**

Thank God for You

COLOSSIANS 1:1-8

AIM

To learn positive ways of encouraging faith and discipleship.

BEGIN HERE

Think of something (or someone!) in the life of the local church for which you feel particularly thankful. Share your thanks, preferably in small groups.

BIBLE STUDY

READ COLOSSIANS 1:1-8

Introduction

Trouble was never far away in the life of the early Church. Most of Paul's letters were prompted by problems of one sort or another. The church in Colossae was getting into difficulties. False teaching was beginning to creep in; helping the church to confront this problem was Paul's major reason for writing the letter. Later in it, he is going to have to correct those who have swerved from their simple faith in Jesus. But things at Colossae are not all negative and so he begins on a note of encouragement. He addresses the Colossian Christians as 'the holy and faithful brothers in Christ' (1:2). 'This is what you are,' he is saying, 'holy, set apart, different from others because of your faith in Christ.' He goes on to spell out how thankful he is to God for all that he has heard about the church in Colossae (1: 3-4). He writes of their 'faith and love that spring from the hope that is stored up for you in heaven' (1: 5) and later he speaks of their 'love in the Spirit' (1:8).

>> Now look at Question 1.

He then makes an indirect reference to two kinds of false teaching which prompted the letter. He writes of the 'word of truth' (1:5), clearly stating that he knows they have heard what is true — the truth of the good news of Jesus Christ. This contrasts with 'the human tradition' and 'the hollow and deceptive philosophy' of the heretical teaching they are now hearing (2:8). The hallmark of this false teaching was that it suggested truth was exclusive — reserved for the spiritual elite who were thought to have special understanding. In contrast Paul writes that 'all over the world this gospel is bearing fruit and growing' (1:6) and he speaks of 'God's grace' as being the heart of the gospel message.

The possibility of being saved by observing religious practices was one part of the false teaching the Colossians were hearing. Someone has said that this is still the most widespread misunderstanding about the Christian faith. We all know people who believe that right relationship with God is a matter of doing the right things, saying the right words and praying the right prayers. Paul, however, speaks of God's grace as being the heart of the gospel message. The hard-to-grasp truth is, of course, that the gospel is the good news of forgiveness and new life achieved for us by Jesus Christ. The gospel message is about grace.

>> Now look at Question 2.

Paul speaks of the way that Epaphras had made sure that the Colossians had not only heard the good news of Jesus but understood what it meant to follow him. Jesus' great commission was to 'make disciples of all nations, ... teaching them to obey everything I have commanded you' (Matthew 28:19-20) . Discipleship goes much deeper than an initial decision to follow Jesus. It demands a whole change in our way of thinking and living. There are choices to be made.

>> Now look at Questions 3 and 4.

So in these opening verses of this letter, Paul's message of encouragement to the believers is this: they have put their trust in Jesus, the true way to God, and he wants them to realize and be thankful that their life as a church is bearing fruit.

>> See Action

Questions

1. What can we learn from the way in which Paul begins his letter about the role of encouragement within the church? Make a list of practical ways in which you can encourage others in your church.

2. How do we sometimes make the gospel message one of bad news of condemnation, making those both inside and outside the church feel that they must earn their salvation? How would you help someone to grasp the truth of the good news that salvation is a free gift?

3. How would you put in your own words what it means to be a disciple? (Perhaps you could imagine you were trying to explain it to a non church-going teenage student studying for his exams in Religious Studies!)

4. Are there areas in your life which are off-limits to God? Ask group members to think about personal 'no go' areas from which God is excluded, or maybe simply not very welcome. Then discuss ways in which you can be more open to God. What do you think is the most positive thing we can do to help another Christian be a better disciple?

ACTION

Paul used prayer and thanksgiving to encourage others as they sought to follow Jesus.

As a group make a record of prayer and thanksgiving which will help you to encourage others in the church. You might use a scrapbook, with lists on alternate pages of thanksgivings (even in situations which appear difficult at first sight) and of intercessions. Leave room to note down what happens after you begin to pray. Arrange for one person to look after the book, bring it to each meeting and keep it up to date. You may want to include pictures or symbols to keep it looking interesting. Be creative!

Make sure you have a way of keeping in contact between meetings (perhaps by having a phone chain) so that you can keep each other informed of prayer needs and thanksgivings.

Thank God for You

ALTERNATIVE METHOD OF STUDY

This week's alternative method is **Character Study**. Begin the session by dividing the group up to search out all the clues in these verses about Paul, the Colossians, Timothy and Epaphras. They could supplement the search by looking at other passages in the New Testament or at Bible reference books (but beware of doing an exhaustive study of Paul!). Prepare a short biography of a chosen character or a 'mini profile' of the Colossian church. This will give you a good background understanding for looking at the rest of the letter. Go on to use the discussion questions and / or some of the additional questions.

ADDITIONAL QUESTIONS

1. An apostle is defined as 'one who is sent'. Why does Paul emphasise his role as an apostle in verse 1? Is there any difference between his apostleship and that of the twelve apostles? Why should we pay attention to the things he writes in letters such as this?

2. Are there practical ways in which we can follow Paul's example in praying for others?

3. What is the relationship between faith, hope and love? What difference do they make in everyday living?

4. Why is it important that the gospel story is historically accurate? Do the historic facts matter or is it our experience of Christ which really counts?

5. What convinced Paul that the gospel was spreading? What similar evidence do we have in today's world? How can we share in Paul's enthusiasm for the way the gospel message was spreading?

6. What were the ways in which you heard and received the gospel? Are there any lessons to be learned about how we help people to understand the gospel message when they have not heard it before?

BIBLE NOTES

1:1-2 It is often helpful when studying a book of the Bible to understand something of the setting in which it was written. The introductory verses give us the opportunity to answer some important questions.

Did Paul write Colossians? Because of differences of style and use of language from Paul's other letters, some scholars are uncertain about its authorship. There is, however, little doubt that Paul wrote the letter to Philemon and the close association of these two letters gives added weight to the belief that this letter was also written by Paul. The differences may well be explained by the fact that Paul was writing to a people he had never met and, because he was refuting false teaching, his vocabulary picked up some of the phrases of that teaching as he compared it with the gospel.

Why does Paul call himself an apostle? The apostles were men who had been selected by Jesus, from among those who followed him, to be his closest companions. He himself taught them and then sent them out with the commission to teach others. He appeared to them after the resurrection and continued to teach them until his ascension. So how can Paul claim to be an apostle? Simply because he, too, experienced a unique resurrection appearance of Jesus when he was on the road to Damascus, and the church recognized that he had a special commission from Jesus to go and preach to the Gentiles.

Why was the letter written? Paul was writing to help Christians refute teaching that undermined their faith. Among the competing philosophies current in Colossae was Gnosticism. *Gnosis* is the Greek word for knowledge: our word 'agnostic' means one who believes that nothing beyond the material world may be known with certainty. Also the Gnostics claimed to have special knowledge. Their teaching gave great importance to other spiritual powers in the universe besides Jesus. This, together with the idea that the rigorous observance of religious practice would lead to spiritual perfection, undermined the place of Jesus and his sacrifice on the cross and took away the freedom from the Law that Jesus brings.

What do we know about Colossae? Colossae was situated near the modern town of Denizli in Western Turkey, about 100 miles from the coastal town of Ephesus, in the region of the seven churches mentioned in Revelation. It was on the main trade route from the East and, not surprisingly, the people were a diverse ethnic mixture of native Colossians, Greeks and Jews. There were differing cultural and religious ideas; it was an ideal place for false teaching to take root! The city, once large and wealthy, was declining in importance; nearby Laodicea was the seat of Roman administration and the spa town of Hierapolis was the centre of culture. Soon after the letter was written, the area was struck by a major earthquake. Laodicea was rebuilt but Colossae was never restored. The site remains uninhabited and unexcavated.

1:4 Paul had never visited Colossae himself, but we are told in Acts that during his extended ministry in Ephesus, 'all the Jews and Greeks who lived in the province of Asia heard the word of the Lord' (Acts 19:10). We can assume that travellers to Ephesus would have taken news back and forth from the nearby region and so, in this way, Paul would have heard of this church.

1:7 Epaphras was a native of Colossae and it is thought that he (and possibly Philemon as well) had heard Paul preach at Ephesus. He not only took the gospel back to his home town but was also concerned for the churches in Hierapolis and Laodicea (see 4:13). It is also possible that he may have been imprisoned for his faith (see Philemon 23).

WORSHIP AND PRAYER

Have a time of thanksgiving (we have so much for which to be thankful!) and pray for those whose lives are lacking in joy.

Pray for those in your group, thanking God for the good things you see in each other. Don't be afraid to be specific — you might find you encourage one another!

Pray that God will use you as individuals and as a church to bring the good news of God's forgiveness to those among whom you live. You might like to pray in silence for one particular person — asking for the special sensitivity to be a witness to God's forgiveness through Jesus. Or pray that you might be able to help a fellow-believer understand more fully what it means to be one of Jesus' disciples.
›› See Sunday Extra on page 36 for ideas for songs and hymns.

2

Group Sheet

The Will to Live

COLOSSIANS 1:9-20

 AIM To learn how we can follow God's will for our lives.

 BEGIN HERE Think of some everyday situations where accurate knowledge is important for right actions. Why are the two connected?

 BIBLE STUDY
READ COLOSSIANS 1:9-20

 Introduction
Prayer matters! Paul's letters show that he prayed not only for the church in Colossae but in other places too. Here Paul prays that the Christians in Colossae will have the knowledge of God's will and of two particular gifts of the Spirit — wisdom and understanding. These were essential in the spiritual battle against the insidious false teaching which offered possession of special knowledge. The Holy Spirit can enable us to separate out what is true from what is false. He can also help us to understand God's will for our lives so that daily we can choose to go his way.
>> Now look at Question 1.

Paul then goes on to explain the reason for his prayer (1:10). Contrary to the suggestions of the false teachers of Colossae, knowledge is not an end in itself. It affects how we live our everyday lives. We need to understand God's will, so that we live in a way that pleases him and work for him productively. We need God's dynamic power to do that (1:11). This is not worldly power, which would lord it over others, but the power of God demonstrated by Jesus, which stands firm in the face of trouble and enables us to hold on to our faith, 'joyfully giving thanks to the Father' (1:12). It's the kind of joy which, as Jesus promised, can be experienced despite situations which are causing pain (John 16:20).
>> Now look at Questions 2 and 3.

The false teachers claimed that men and women could earn their own salvation. In contrast Paul puts the good news in a nutshell (1:13). God rescued us from the rule of evil forces in the world, when we were unable to save ourselves; he took us from under Satan's rule, released us from slavery and transported us into Jesus' kingdom where we are forgiven.

It is likely that the false teaching being given at Colossae also claimed (like many of today's cults and religions) that Jesus was one among many ways to God. Paul explains exactly who Jesus is:

* *he is not just like God; he is the exact representation of God in every detail (1:15);*
* *he was there in the beginning, he designed and made everything, rules over all and by his*

power the universe continues to exist (1:16-18);
- *he guides and directs the Church (1:18);*
- *he is everything that is God (1:19);*
- *he brings everything into harmony with God (1:20).*

>> Now look at Question 4.

Questions

1. Make a list of the circumstances in which you might need the spiritual gifts of wisdom or understanding.

How can you know, when you receive these gifts, that they are from God? Think of three ways in which you can test your gifts. Has there been a time in your life when you have been aware of God giving you one of these gifts? What is the role of 'sanctified common sense'?

2. Can you think of at least four ways in which we can come to know God's will in our lives?

3. Have you had a personal experience of God's power helping you keep faith at a time when you found it hard to follow him? Share your experiences.

4. Why do you believe in Jesus? Try to pinpoint three things that have helped you to faith; it may help you to write them down. Talk about them in pairs or small groups.

How are the points that Paul makes about Jesus in verses 13-20 important as we talk to people around us about our faith?

ACTION

We have read about the power of God which can transform our lives and about Jesus as Lord, who should rule our lives.

Singly or in pairs look at the list below and mark three areas of your life where you want to see God's power at work.

Use of time:	*at home*	*at work*	*in worship*	*for others*
Relationships with:	*family*	*friends*	*your children*	*colleagues*
Use of talents:	*DIY*	*music*	*art*	*cooking*
Use of money to:	*spend*	*invest*	*give to God*	*give to others*
Thought life:	*reading*	*watching (TV/films/videos)*	*relaxation*	*planning*

Other:

Highlight just one of these and pray today for God's power in that area. Keep a note of it and watch for God to answer your prayer. If you do this as pairs then you could agree to pray for one another during the next two weeks.

The Will to Live

ALTERNATIVE METHOD OF STUDY

This week's suggested method is the use of **Key Questions**, such as those used for many years in the Scripture Union Bible reading notes. These help you look for ideas in a passage and can be a very useful standby when you are short of time for preparation! You will not find answers to all the questions in every passage, but this section of Colossians has something to discover in response to most of the questions. The Key Questions are:

1. What is this passage basically about?

2. What does it teach about God the Father; his Son, Jesus Christ our Lord; the Holy Spirit?

3. What does it teach about life? Is there a command, a promise, a warning, an example to follow, an error to avoid?

ADDITIONAL QUESTIONS

1. What picture of growing in Christian maturity is portrayed in verses 9-11? In what areas should our lives be changing?

2. How is our growth in character linked to our relationship to God?

3. What are the various ways in which verses 12 and 13 describe the nature of God's rescue of mankind? What difference has this rescue made to you?

4. How is Jesus' relationship to the universe described in verses 15-17?

5. If Jesus is head of the Church (1:18), how can we let him be in charge of its life?

6. What do verses 15-20 tell us about the way in which Jesus reveals God to us?

BIBLE NOTES

1:9 Paul seems to have prayed regularly and systematically for others. Constant prayer may also be the sort of thing Paul writes about to the Romans, when he refers to the Spirit who helps us when we do not know how to pray and who 'intercedes ... with groans that words cannot express ... for the saints in accordance with God's will' (Romans 8:26,27). While much else was going on around them, he and Timothy may well have experienced the activity of the Holy Spirit within them constantly interceding for the Christians at Colossae.

1:11 In this verse Paul uses the Greek words *dunamoo* which, in the New International Version is translated 'strengthened', and *dunamis* (translated 'power'). These are the root words for our words 'dynamite' and 'dynamic'. They suggest that nothing can stand against God's power.

1:13 Only those who cannot save themselves need to be rescued and, having been rescued, they are taken to a place of safety, the kingdom of the Son. Redemption is the purchase of freedom for a slave.

1:15 Jesus is the image of God, an exact portrayal. Jesus said: 'If you really knew me, you would know my Father as well' (John 14:7).

1:16-18 Jesus is spoken of as the creator, ruler and sustainer of the universe — not the first of many created beings but the one who began the creation and was given a place of honour above it. Everything was made by him and for him, including the array of angelic beings which the false teachers claimed to be in a hierarchy of powers between God and man, and of which they claimed Jesus was only one.

Paul speaks of everything being held together in Jesus. The laws of science are discoveries made by men and women. But often the reasons behind those laws remain a mystery. Paul says it is the power of the one for whom and through whom the universe was made, which holds everything together.

1:18 This verse speaks of Jesus as the head of the Church. The head is the part of the body that has control. Paul speaks of Jesus as the beginning or *arche* (the root of our word 'architect', someone who designs something and makes sure it conforms to the design).

1:19 All that is God, all the divine qualities, have made their home in Jesus. (The word used is *katiokeo* meaning to settle down, or make a permanent home.)

1:20 Paul speaks of everything being reconciled to God. This need not imply that everyone is ultimately saved, rather that everything takes its rightful place in God's plan for the universe. The word 'reconcile' can be understood to include the admission by the evil powers of the rightful place of Jesus. That idea is borne out elsewhere in the New Testament when we are told that 'at the name of Jesus every knee should bow.' (Philippians 2:10)

WORSHIP AND PRAYER

Have a time of praise worshipping Jesus for who he is (perhaps using the words in Colossians 1:15-20). Follow this with a time of thanksgiving for all he has done in rescuing us from Satan's power and in equipping us to follow him.

Join together in a prayer of commitment, asking Jesus to take first place in our lives. Be sensitive to those in the group who may not have had a previous opportunity to pray in this way.

Pray for one another (maybe in twos or threes) asking God to give you his gifts of wisdom and understanding in any difficult situations you face this week. (These may not be ones you can foresee!)
>> **See Sunday Extra** on page 36-37 for ideas for songs and hymns.

3

Group Sheet

Secure Faith

COLOSSIANS 1:21 - 2:5

AIM
To learn how to help one another to Christian faith and maturity.

BEGIN HERE
Think of one time in your life when you found your faith shaken — perhaps when you felt let down by someone or by God. Tell the person next to you about your experience and about how you coped with it.

BIBLE STUDY
READ COLOSSIANS 1:21 - 2:5

Introduction
The Christian life is not always plain sailing. Occasionally unexpected gusts threaten to blow us off course. It may be a flurry of incorrect ideas, such as those the church in Colossae faced or it might be a gale of difficult circumstances, such as those Paul experienced. Both can challenge the security we should have in our relationship with God. These are issues that Paul addresses in this passage.

The false teachers in Colossae may well have tried to sow seeds of doubt in the minds of the Christians about the validity of their faith. So Paul reminds his listeners why it was they became Christians. He uses forceful language to help them remember that they had not merely been separated from God but, by their actions and attitudes, they had been actively working against him (1:21). Through Epaphras they had heard the 'word of truth' (1:5) and had been reconciled to God.

›› Now look at Question 1.

He then reminds them that Jesus offers complete forgiveness (1:22). Just as he used strong language to emphasise the depth of separation from God, Paul makes it clear that the work of Christ on the cross is complete. He utterly refutes the idea that we still need to earn our salvation or to make up for the past. Paul makes it clear that, when we become Christians, God makes us his and says to us, as Jesus said to the woman caught in the act of adultery: 'Neither do I condemn you' (John 8:11). He speaks of God as the one who reconciles, making it clear that it is God who takes the initiative.

›› Now look at Question 2.

Paul then paints a picture of faith in Jesus being built on a foundation that cannot be shaken (1:23). Colossae is in an area prone to earthquakes so the picture of unshakeable foundations would have had its appeal!

›› Now look at Question 3.

The Colossian Christians were under pressure, but in telling them of his own situation, Paul reminds them of the richness of faith in Jesus. Paul was suffering, but was glad to do so as an unavoidable part of sharing the world's rejection of Jesus (1:24). He also had a commission to fulfil: to preach the message that Jesus lives in us, giving hope both now and for the life to come (1: 25-27). His concern is to bring people to Christian maturity (1:28). He makes it clear that, even though they are virtual strangers (2:1), his love for the Colossian Christians means that he is using all the energy God has given him (1:29) to make sure that they have a full understanding of their faith (2:2). He knows that if he can help them have a real understanding of the love of God in Jesus, they will be strengthened and drawn closer to one another (2:2). They will know that Jesus is all they need (2:3) and so be able to stand against the persuasive talk of the heretics (2:4-5).

›› Now look at Question 4.

Questions

1. Who has been important to you in your journey of faith? Write a list and then, in pairs, tell each other about one of those people, and about the impact he or she made on you. Which one quality would you like to have, in order to help others to faith?

2. People say: 'Jesus was a remarkable man and great teacher — but why all this business about him being God?' How would you start explaining to a friend that Jesus is fully human and fully God? Spend a few minutes working out your response. In pairs take two minutes each to explain what you would say.

3. What qualities make a person dependable? List the characteristics which make you feel you can completely trust someone. Do you see these in Jesus? Tell the story of one time when you have found Jesus to be dependable.

4. How would you describe a mature Christian? What characteristics of such a person can you see in this passage? How does maturity affect our relationship to God and other people?

ACTION

What concerns, shown in this passage by Paul for the Colossian Christians, do we need to show for fellow Christians today? List them below. How can you go about this, especially in the life of your group?

_____

_____

_____

_____

_____

_____

Group Sheet

3

Secure Faith

ALTERNATIVE METHOD OF STUDY

Try **Analysing the Chapter** this week. Give everyone a copy of the passage, or a piece of paper on which they can make their own notes. Ask them to divide the passage up into chunks and to write a newspaper-style heading which sums up the message of each one. Finally, provide an overall title for the passage. Compare your headings in small groups (perhaps deciding which best sums things up). This is a good method to encourage people to get to the heart of what a passage is saying.

ADDITIONAL QUESTIONS

1. Paul pulls no punches in his description of life lived in separation from God (1:21). Did you experience alienation from God before you came to faith in Christ? How do Paul's words affect your attitude to your non-Christian friends?

2. It's said that, as far as religion is concerned, we now live in a 'pick and mix' culture. People are free to assemble their own personal combination of beliefs from a variety of sources. With that in mind, what aspects of this passage would help as you try to explain the gospel to friends and neighbours?

3. What does this passage tell us about God's ultimate goal for his people? How does Christ make this goal possible? How can we help each other make progress toward that goal now?

4. Paul speaks of suffering and of struggling (1:24 - 2:5). How does being a Christian lead to particular problems and dilemmas? Make a list of some of the things which encourage us to keep going in spite of problems. What for you makes the Christian life worth living?

5. What do these verses tell of the costliness of Christian ministry? Is Christian service an easy option today? How can you support those involved in ministry?

6. What characteristics does Paul want to see in the life of the church (2:2-5)? Why are they important? What can you do to strengthen the unity within your church and with Christians in other churches?

BIBLE NOTES

1:22 Paul emphasises the 'physical body' of Jesus. He was a real flesh-and-blood man. Some of the Colossian heresy may have involved trying to 'spiritualise' the gospel and make out that Jesus' death and resurrection were not actual happenings.

1:23 The use of the word 'if' is a warning not to turn from faith. Along with the warning comes a picture of a faith that is totally unshakeable. The word 'established' means to lay a foundation and 'firm' means settled (as in a building). In an area where earthquakes were common, the idea of firm foundations would have had clear meaning.

The reference to the gospel being proclaimed to every creature is a dramatic way of making the point that the gospel is a universal message about a God who has reconciled the world to himself.

1:24 When Paul speaks of 'what is still lacking in regard to Christ's afflictions', he does not mean that what Jesus did on the cross was incomplete; he has already made clear (1:20) that the work of Jesus is all-encompassing. It is possible that he has in mind the words of Jesus about the suffering which the Church, as the community of the Messiah, must experience before his return (Matthew 24:21-22). In his affliction Paul was taking upon himself some measure of that suffering.

1:25 Paul's suffering is the direct consequence of bringing the good news of Jesus to the Gentiles, the job which God has given him.

1:26-27 This 'mystery' is not something hidden. Now, since the coming of Christ, it is revealed to all. The 'mystery' is that God's plan of salvation includes Gentiles as well as Jews. Christ's presence with them is the guarantee of the future glory which will be theirs.

1:28-29 Paul's concern for people does not end when they come to faith, only when they are presented to Christ at his coming, mature and fruitful. Such work can only be done with Christ's help.

CHAPTER 2
2:2-4 The false teachers were offering special, rarefied knowledge and wisdom. Paul says that Christ is the source of all the wisdom we need. He wants the church to grow in understanding the truth, but also in love and unity to stand firm against false teaching.

2:5: The words 'orderly' and 'firm' are words which were used in a military context. They would have conveyed the meaning of not breaking ranks in the face of attack.

WORSHIP AND PRAYER
Thank God for all the ways in which he has made himself known in your life. Pray for those who helped to bring you to faith in Jesus.

Pray for the person on either side of you — that he or she may always know the forgiveness that is theirs through Jesus and may know him to be a dependable friend.

Ask God to draw together in love all the churches in your area and to show you how you can together stand firm in the faith. Pray for any you know who are suffering because of their faith. (School can occasionally be a challenging environment for children from Christian homes. Pray for children of group members. If your minister has children at school, you might include them in this prayer — it can be particularly tough being 'the vicar's kid'.)

Pray for yourselves as a group, that each of you might be given an opportunity this week to witness to your faith. Ask God to make the opportunity clear and to give you the wisdom and understanding to communicate what you believe with clarity and sensitivity.
>> See Sunday Extra on page 37 for ideas for songs and hymns.

4 **Group Sheet**

Set Free

COLOSSIANS 2:6-23

AIM
To learn to live life by trusting in Christ, not by obeying rules.

BEGIN HERE
In groups of two or three, ask people to try and remember some of their school rules. What were those rules trying to achieve (apart, of course, from misery, frustration and ingenious ways around them)? Were they successful? Were they all necessary? What happened if you broke them?

BIBLE STUDY
READ COLOSSIANS 2:6-23

Introduction
There is a saying attributed to St Augustine: 'Love God and do what you like.' Paul could well have used it to sum up what he wanted to say to the Colossians in this part of his letter. As a Pharisee, he had once been the willing prisoner of strict regulations. Now he longs for his fellow-Christians to know that following Jesus frees them from similar obsessive rule-keeping. He reminds them that, having acknowledged Jesus as their Lord, they need to live out their original profession of faith (2:6). For a Christian there are no half measures, either Jesus is Lord of our lives or he is not; rules and regulations must not take his place.

>> Now look at Question 1.

Paul goes on to paint a series of brief word pictures of the Christian life (2:7). It is 'rooted' in Jesus, like a healthy plant growing in the right spot. It is being 'built up', like a building rising from solid foundations. It is also described as being 'strengthened', which some translations put as 'established', so that our relationship to God is as secure as a signed treaty which cannot be changed. Lastly it is 'overflowing' with thanksgiving, like a brim-full container with its contents pouring over the top.

>> Now look at Question 2.

In contrast, in the next verse (2:8) there is a picture of being carried off, like the plunder of battle, by false teaching, which Paul calls 'hollow' and 'deceptive'. He warns the Colossians that these teachings were based on human philosophies and not on the God-given revelation of faith in Jesus. In him alone the whole nature of the Godhead is present (2:9); he gives us all we need for Christian living (2:10).

>> Now look at Question 3.

The next section of the letter contrasts the life offered by Jesus with the now obsolete traditions of the Jewish faith. Baptism, not circumcision, is now the sign of belonging to the people of God. It is also a sign of the Christian's identification with the death and resurrection of Jesus,

who alone puts us right with God (2:11-12). Those who were once separated from him are raised into glorious, new life with Jesus, who bore the penalty for our law-breaking in his death on the cross (2:13-14). His death is also like a victory parade over all the spiritual powers (2:15).
>> Now look at Question 4.

Paul helps the Colossians take a look at the rules and regulations which would take away their new-found freedom (2:16). He wants them to realize that, like the Jewish Law, they were a shadow compared to the real thing: an imperfect image of the reality brought by Jesus (2:17). He tells them that the rigid observance of any such laws will bring them into a position of slavery — something that God does not intend. Paul urges the Christians to stand firm in the freedom of Jesus and not to be cheated of it by the teachers of a cult religion, who have deceived themselves (2:18) and in reality are like limbs disconnected from the body because they have let go of Jesus (2:19). Paul asks them to look at these regulations from the standpoint of their new faith. The apparently attractive order and discipline they offer were really only a means of self-gratification (2:23).
>> See Action.

Questions

1. In what ways do we still imprison ourselves with spiritual rules and regulations? Ask everyone to think of at least one example of how we do this as individuals and as a church. Are there any ways in which our attitudes can change to reflect the freedom we are given by Jesus?

Are any rules essential to the living out of our Christian faith? Make a list of those rules people feel are necessary, without commenting on them. Then go on to discuss whether these rules are important or not.

2. How do Paul's word pictures help us understand the Christian life? Do you experience the vibrancy that Paul describes here? (You might like individually to draw a sketch or write a word picture of your relationship with Jesus and then discuss it in small groups.)

3. What do you need to sustain your faith? Together compile a list of things which help you. Now imagine that you have been imprisoned for your faith and have nothing in your cell apart from a mattress. Cross off from the list the things you are denied. What do you have left? How well do you think your faith would survive?

4. How does baptism give us a picture of what Christ has done for us? How does it give us a picture of what Christian living is about? How can we put into practice what our baptism signifies?

ACTION

How can we live out our belief that we can do nothing apart from Jesus? Ask everyone to write a list of things they tend to do in their own strength. In order to discuss practical ways in which you can begin to rely more on Jesus, think of at least three ways in which children show that they trust their parents. How can we reflect this trust by the way we live our lives as children of God?

Group Sheet 4

Set Free

ALTERNATIVE METHOD OF STUDY

This week try the **Swedish Method** of study. Give everyone a piece of paper with these three symbols on it: a candle, a question mark and an arrow. Ask them to read the passage and jot down against each symbol the number of at least one verse. Against the *candle* they are to jot down the number of a verse which has brought new light and inspiration, perhaps teaching something fresh or bringing encouragement. Against the *question mark* list a verse you don't understand. Against the *arrow* put verses which may have pricked your conscience, demanding a response or action.

ADDITIONAL QUESTIONS

1. How should our Christian living build on our initial commitment to Christ (2:6-7)?

2. What might be the present-day equivalent of the false ideas and cults (2:8) which lead people astray? How are many of them similar in approach to the false teaching outlined here? How do you tell that something does not agree with Christian teaching?

3. How does our view of Christ make a difference to how we live the Christian life?

4. How does the death and resurrection of Jesus set us free and change our lives (2:11-15)?

5. Why do we almost instinctively seek to lead our lives by codes of rules and laws? How does doing so make us feel good (2:16-23)? How should Christians view rules and regulations? Why do they ultimately not satisfy?

6. What sort of freedom should Christians demonstrate? Can we just do as we please?

BIBLE NOTES

2:6 The Greek word translated here as 'receive' is a technical term used for receiving and accepting a handed-on tradition. Paul points out a uniquely Christian truth. We do not inherit the kind of legalistic attitude to God which Paul had defended in his days as a Pharisee. Neither do we inherit the rituals and rules of a religion of human origins, like the Colossian cult-followers. In fact, we don't inherit any *thing*. We inherit a *person* — Christ himself. The Christian acknowledges Christ as Lord in baptism and must then make good that profession of faith by living with Jesus as Lord.

2:7 The Greek word for 'rooted' is *rhizoomai*, from which we get the word 'rhizome' — a root stock. 'Strengthened' may also be translated as 'established', meaning to be confirmed or ratified as with a legal contract. Both images give a picture of the security we have in our relationship with Jesus.

2:8 Paul knew from his own experience that the revelation of Jesus came directly from God. He warns the Colossians against being captured (literally, carried off as slaves) by 'hollow and deceptive philosophies'. He uses this description because the false teachers were caught up in the love of wisdom, based on 'human tradition' — a philosophy handed down from one person to another and not from God. The New International Version translates the next phrase as an amplification of this and refers to the 'basic principles of this world'. The original Greek uses the word *stoicheia* which could mean 'elementary things' of this world, hence the New International Version translation. But it could also mean the 'elements', in terms of the spirits or demonic powers which seek to rival Christ. Paul uses the word in that sense elsewhere and most other translations take it to be the meaning here.

2:9-10 Jesus possesses all the nature and attributes (the 'fullness') of God, so there is no place for other intermediary beings to come between us and God. We have a share of that 'fulness' as we belong to Christ and share his life. We do not need any other experiences or spiritual disciplines. All we need has been given to us in Christ.

2:12-13 Paul talks first about circumcision (2:11) and then about baptism (2:12). The former was intended as the sign of the covenant between God and his chosen people. But many in Israel had come to believe that the physical operation of removing the foreskin was actually a means to a right relationship with God instead of being simply the sign of it. For the Christians, baptism was the sign of belonging to God's people and also of being identified with the death and resurrection of Jesus. The truth of this is made even clearer by the fact that Paul uses the terms 'co-buried' , 'co-raised' and 'co-quickened' (translated in 2:13 as 'alive with Christ'). So, through faith and baptism, we receive the new life which Christ has made possible.

2:14 Translators differ as to the meaning of the first half of this verse which speaks of either a 'bond' or a 'legal code'. The Greek refers to a legal document, which could be our undertaking to obey the law (hence 'bond') or possibly the law itself. Either way it points to our failure to live up to God's standards! The second half of the verse pictures the way the crimes of someone crucified were listed on a placard nailed to the cross — it was for all *our* crimes that Jesus died.

2:15 The picture here is of the sort of victory procession in which the conquering general was followed by all the disarmed enemies — from kings to foot-soldiers — who had been taken captive. Christ has conquered all the supernatural powers which oppose him.

2:16-17 By his victory Jesus brought freedom not only from slavery to sin but also from the tyranny of rules and regulations by which we tell ourselves that we can earn our own salvation. Jesus himself said that he had not come to do away with the Law — a law which God gave to mankind — but to fulfil it by carrying it out in the spirit in which it was given.

2:18 By recounting visions, to back up what they teach, these people may seem 'super spiritual'.

2:21-23 In Romans (14 and 15) Paul refers to dietary laws and explains that people will have different ideas about what they should eat and what they should drink. But he makes clear that the important thing is that we should honour the Lord in everything we do, neither judging others nor causing them to stumble by our actions.

WORSHIP AND PRAYER

Read Psalm 98 aloud. Use it as a basis for thanksgiving for God's gift of freedom, our salvation. You could read it straight through, but it might be more helpful to use different voices for each paragraph. It may also be helpful to stop at intervals for open prayer.

Pray for those who live in the shadow of fear. They may include those known to you personally, as well as those in difficult situations around the world. Pray for the spread of God's light.

Pray for yourself and for your Church, that you may be continually open to the leading of the Holy Spirit, ready to accept change, not bound by man-made traditions but living an unshackled life of faith.
>> See Sunday Extra on page 38 for ideas for songs and hymns.

5

Group Sheet

All Change

COLOSSIANS 3:1-17

AIM
To realize that Jesus offers the possibility of a completely new way of life.

BEGIN HERE
How do you feel when you put on new clothes? Excited? Delighted? Disappointed? Choose four words to describe your feelings. Do they echo your attitude to becoming or being a Christian?

BIBLE STUDY
READ COLOSSIANS 3:1-17

Introduction
When we become Christians we do not become puppets. God isn't in the business of pulling our strings. Instead we continue to have to choose day by day whether or not to allow Jesus to transform our lives. Paul begins this part of his letter by calling on us to live as people who share Christ's risen life (3:1). This will involve choices about how we live our lives and about what motivates us as we do so (3:2). Paul encourages us to do this by standing firm in what we have been taught: that we have died to our former way of life (3:3) and that in time we will be seen to share in the glory of Jesus (3:4).
>> Now look at Question 1.

At creation God gave mankind free will. Our story since then shows the result of repeatedly choosing our way, not his. Paul gives two ugly lists of offences which belong to our fallen nature. He makes it clear that sin is a reality that will not go away. He wants Christians to understand that while they have become a new creation through faith in Jesus, they need to continue exercising their free will in choosing to turn away from a life dominated by sin (3:5,7,8a). Paul encourages us to recognize that it is sin which prevents people from living in freedom. He uses the imagery of 'taking off' the old life and 'putting on' the new as if a worn-out garment were being replaced with a fresh one. But this is not simply an instantaneous change; it's a progressive transformation (3:10). It won't all happen overnight and, of course, the fact that Christ is renewing his people will affect their relationships with one another (3:11).
>> Now look at Question 2.

As we seek to follow God's way we are not left to do things in our own strength. God gives us all the help we need. He loves us and has made us his chosen people (3:12). He offers us the 'new clothing' of the different way of life of those whom Jesus sets free from sin (3:12-14).
>> Now look at Question 3.

It's not just a matter of individual transformation. This gradual change will be seen in the life of the whole church. The peace which comes from our unity in Christ will shape the life of the community, as will our thankfulness for all God has done for us. We must absorb Jesus' teaching so that it becomes an integral part of us, so that our speech and actions in every situation reflect

his character (3:17). This is something in which we can help one another, by teaching and correction, exercising wisdom and love as we do so, and by our worship together.
>> Now look at Question 4.

Questions

1. How do we seek God's will for our daily lives? Invite group members to think of three regular activities which they tend to do on 'automatic pilot'. How might these be affected if our hearts are set 'on things above' (3:1)?

2. Look at Paul's list of 'basic badness' (3:5-10). What are the 'chains' in our personal backgrounds that might prevent us from living out our faith? Invite each person to think of one 'shackle' and write it down. Some may be willing to share this with the rest of the group; others may prefer to be more private about what they have written. Spend time thinking of practical ways in which Jesus provides freedom from each of these 'chains'.

3. In what ways have the 'new clothes' of life with Christ changed your attitude to work, friendships, money and family relationships?

Write the eight qualities listed in verses 12-14 on cards and distribute them. Ask group members to thinks of real-life ways of completing statements like these: 'Compassion is when...; Kindness is like...'. Share your definitions. How do we learn to show these characteristics in our lives?

4. In verses 15-17 Paul shows the Christian life, individual and communal, as it ought to be. What aspect challenges you most when you think about your own life, and when you think about the life of your church? In which of the areas listed by Paul do you and your church most need to grow? What can you do as a group to encourage this growth in each other and in the church? Set yourselves one personal and one group target.

ACTION

Look at the sins which Paul lists. The first list (3:5) is concerned mainly with the wrong use of our sexuality. It features:

- Wrong sexual relationships,
- Wrong sexual attitudes, thoughts and desires,
- Wrong desires in general and greed (Paul links it with idolatry) in particular.

The second list (3:8-9) is mainly about the wrong things we can say to each other:
- Anger and rage,
- Malice, active ill-will,
- Slander, degrading someone by what you say about him or her,
- Bad language,
- Lying.

Individually note, or mark on the lists, areas in which God has changed you since becoming a Christian. Have you experienced God's forgiveness? Or do you still feel a sense of guilt? Are you able to encourage the rest of the group by sharing how God has helped you? If the group feel able, spend a few minutes sharing experience of these very sensitive areas. Make it clear that no one is under any pressure to 'open up'. Spend time praying for one another.

All Change

ALTERNATIVE METHOD OF STUDY

This week's suggested method is that of **Highlighting** a copy of the passage to bring out its important features. Distribute copies and have available a selection of coloured pens, pencils or highlighters. Ask the group to read through the passage, using different colours to pick out key points, repeated themes and marking such things as links or contrasts. This can be used as a method of study for many passages and is particularly useful for sections of the epistles. Another approach for this particular passage would be to divide a blank sheet into two columns; ask group members to list the 'negatives' of the passage on one side and the 'positives' on the other. Go on to share your findings, particularly looking at the contrasts between the old life and the new.

ADDITIONAL QUESTIONS

1. What does it mean to 'set our minds on things above' (3:1-2)? Is it pie-in-the-sky escapism? How do we establish right perspectives for Christian living?

2. Look at the list of sins Paul gives in verses 5-9. Which of them upsets you most when you see it in others or read about it in the papers? How did Jesus respond to the sin he saw in others? How do you think he reacts to our sin?

3. How do we 'put to death' (3:5) the things which are wrong in our lives? Is this really possible?

4. What does it mean to you to belong to the all-inclusive group Paul describes in verse 11? How should the life of the church reflect this?

5. What are the motives for living the sort of life Paul speaks of in verses 12-14? How do these characteristics all relate to one another?

6. What are the marks of church life outlined in verses 15-17? Why are they important? How do they enable us as individuals to live for God?

BIBLE NOTES

3:1 In the New International Version the chapter begins 'Since, then, you have been raised with Christ.' It is a confident statement of our Christian status. Some translations begin with the word 'if', which may cause confusion if it is taken to imply some doubt about our relationship to Christ.

3:2 Paul tells the Christians to 'set their hearts on things above'. He knows that they need to be determined to live with Jesus as their motivating force, and then they will act according to his will. But if their thinking is on an earthly plane then they will act according to the ways of this world.

3:3-4 Paul speaks of Christians having died with Christ, echoing the free-will commitment made in baptism. He speaks of their life now being 'hidden' in Jesus, using the Greek idiom for death to show that, just as in death the body is hidden in the earth, so now, through baptism, the person that they were is dead and buried in Jesus. The word 'hidden' also conveyed the fact that this new life was not recognized by the world. But Paul makes it clear that believers will be vindicated when Jesus returns, because not only will Christ be seen, but the Christians will also be seen sharing his glory.

3:5 The sins in this list are mainly to do with the wrong use of our sexuality. Sexual immorality (or 'fornication') refers to voluntary sexual intercourse between people who are not married (or not married to each other). Impurity refers to moral uncleanness, or obscenity. Lust is the 'animal desire for sexual indulgence' which may lead to sexual excess or perversion. Evil desires and greed (or covetousness) may apply to material possessions or sexuality; one is yearning for things that are wrong, and the other a craving for things we cannot have. All of these, of course, must be seen in the light of Jesus' challenging 'opening up' of issues of sexual morality (Matthew 5:27-30).

3:8-9 These sins are to do with the verbal abuse of relationships. Anger and rage are violent fits of bad temper. Malice is evil speaking, or active ill-will. Slander means to degrade or debase another by what you say about him or her. Filthy language is indecent talk or vulgar humour. Lying is any attempt to deceive.

3:10 Paul says clearly to the Christians that they need to make sure that their old nature is dead, to be constantly alert to the fact of sin and to live out their new life in Christ.

3:12 Paul uses Old Testament terms for the people of God — chosen, holy and dearly loved — to describe the Church.

Compassion is a deeply felt sympathy for those in need; not a passing emotion, but a way of thinking that results in action. Kindness is a generous interest in and regard for others. Humility is not to be self-deprecating, but to have a proper perspective of your self-worth in God's sight, enabling you to look at others in the same way. Gentleness (the opposite of stormy, harsh, or rude) is not to be confused with weakness. Patience, or long-suffering, is the ability to endure another's wrong conduct without resorting to resentment, the desire for revenge or uncontrolled anger.

3:13 Forbearance and forgiveness complement patience. They are the gifts of withholding judgement and being ready to set free those who have done wrong.

3:14 Love is a selfless emotion, often triggered by an act of will, which puts the well-being of others first. The original Greek speaks of love as 'the bond of perfection'. Some translations take this to mean that love is the bond which unites the church; others, like the New International Version, take it to mean that it is love which binds all the other virtues together and brings them to perfection. The New Testament certainly sees love as the one virtue which sums up all others.

3:15: Here peace is not so much the inner peace Christ gives, but the peace he brings between Christians. The desire to maintain peace must be the determining factor in Christian relationships; ruling, like an umpire, to settle conflicts.

WORSHIP AND PRAYER

Have a look at the list of sins in the **Action** section, then pray in silence asking God to forgive you for those things which you do that are wrong and asking him to help you 'put off' anything of your old nature which is still troubling you.

Read aloud Psalm 40:1-3. Follow this with a time of thanksgiving for the fact that Jesus frees us from slavery to sin.

Either in guided or open prayer ask God to clothe each member of the group with the Christian virtues Paul lists (3:12-14). Pray similarly for the life of your church as a whole for love, forbearance and forgiveness.

›› See Sunday Extra on page 38 for ideas for songs and hymns.

6

Group Sheet

In House

COLOSSIANS 3:18 - 4:1

AIM
To see how Christian discipleship transforms our attitude to those with whom we live and work.

BEGIN HERE
Where do I fit in? Give out sheets of paper. Ask group members each to draw five ladders (or columns on lined paper) with the following headings: world, nation, work, church and home. Next, ask them to fill in the names of those 'over' and 'under' them in each of those structures and to put themselves in what they feel is their correct place. Compare the areas where you are both in, and under, authority.

BIBLE STUDY
READ COLOSSIANS 3:18 - 4:1

Introduction
One mark of a Christian is the ability to see people differently. Paul's teaching challenges the thinking of his culture. He has already written about new attitudes to relationships within the church; he now speaks of how Christians should behave towards those with whom they live and work, some of whom would not be Christians. Looking at this passage is instructive. How do we interpret these fairly bold statements? First, we should note that these are not detailed instructions, just quick 'prods' which Paul makes in passing — correctives, if you like. The picture, perhaps, is as follows: Paul sees families where husbands (even Christian ones) are harsh with their wives and children. Some wives are in a position to challenge their husbands and decide to 'do their own thing' regardless. Children, as children always will, were testing the boundaries.

Paul addresses each member of a household and spells out how he expects God's order to prevail in the homes of Christians. He begins with wives (3:18). He asks them to put themselves willingly under the authority of their husbands. This would not have been a surprising request at a time when women were thought to be less important than men. But Paul turns such thinking on its head when he addresses the husbands (3:19). He writes that a man should love his wife with the love given to him by God and not be harsh or vindictive. The culture in which Paul lived debased women. Paul renounces such attitudes and gives Christian husbands a new idea of the status of women.
>> Now look at Question 1.

Paul then speaks of the relationship between children and parents. He suggests that children (3:20) should give pleasure to the Lord by recognizing their parents' authority. In this way they can fulfil their role within the home and be like Jesus himself who was obedient to his earthly parents (Luke 2.51-52). Paul balances this teaching with instruction to parents on how they should treat their children. He addresses fathers (3:21) as head of the home, but that does not exclude mothers! He asks that they should not cause conflict or discourage their children, by the way they behave towards them, instead they should encourage and support them. Again, this sensitive understanding of children was in marked contrast to contemporary attitudes.

>> Now look at Question 2.

Finally Paul turns to the relationship between slaves and their masters. Slaves were no different, in Jesus' sight, from free men (3:11) but Paul makes a play on words by telling them that they should look on themselves as Jesus' slaves not slaves of their masters (3:24). He reminds them that one day they will inherit God's kingdom and that they are recognized by him as adopted children, not slaves. This will make them interested in doing everything well, not merely when they are being watched (3:23). Paul asks them to respect the authority of their masters (3:22) and to accept their own role within the household. Masters (4:1) should remember that they, too, are slaves of Jesus and should keep this in mind in their treatment of their own slaves. To be just and fair to their slaves would be a far greater witness to the effect of their faith than if they freed them, which would make them homeless and unemployed.

>> Now look at Questions 3 and 4.

Questions

1. What is Paul saying here about relationships in marriage? Is today's view of marriage close to this teaching? Discuss contemporary similarities and differences in each of these areas:
- *the world;*
- *your local community;*
- *the church.*

2. Each think of one child you know well. It may be your own, a neighbour's child or a godchild. Think of one weakness and five strengths of his or her character. How can you use their strengths to give children encouragement? How can you help them overcome their failings?

3. What work paid, unpaid, employed or 'in the home' do you do? Would you say that you
- *see it as work you do for the Lord?*
- *improve your performance when it is likely to be observed?*
- *leave it to God when you feel you are being treated unfairly?*

Discuss these questions in small groups and think of one way in which this passage could help you if you need to change your attitude in any area. (If you are in a position of authority in your work suggest one way in which Paul's words apply to you.)

4. The Church eventually came to see slavery as a social injustice. What similar injustices are there today? Think of examples in your local community; in the nation; in the rest of the world. How could you take action to begin to right one of these injustices?

ACTION

In the light of the passage, are there any changes you would like to make to the way you relate to your marriage partner, family members or work colleagues? Discuss this question in pairs. Decide on two practical changes and two equally practical ways of implementing them.

In House

ALTERNATIVE METHOD OF STUDY

One method of study which we have not yet used is that of **Paraphrasing**. Invite group members to put verses from a passage into their own words, expanding them in the process to bring out their meaning. Ask individuals each to take a section of the passage and rewrite it, covering in turn the relationships of wife / husband, father / child, slave / master. Another approach would be to use Paul's words as the basis for a letter from an 'agony aunt'. Ask the group to imagine a situation to which Paul's words might be addressed today and to write a letter which incorporates his advice. Try to divide the passage between the group so that all the themes are covered.

ADDITIONAL QUESTIONS

1. Is the whole idea of people having authority over others outdated? Why might it have some value? What specifically Christian angle does Paul bring to the idea of order and authority in this passage?

2. What does it mean for a wife to 'submit' to her husband; is it the same as being subservient? What is meant here by husbands loving their wives? How do the two instructions help balance each other?

3. Think of some of the causes of friction within marriage. How can Paul's words make a difference in those specific situations?

4. How might these instructions apply when one of the partners is not a Christian (as would often have been the case among those to whom Paul wrote)? What would be the outcome of following Paul's advice in those situations?

5. What is the picture of family life envisaged in verses 20-21? How do parents sometimes discourage their children? How can parents build a positive relationship with their children?

6. How will it alter our attitude to our work if we recognize that ultimately we are doing it for God? What are the eternal consequences of our behaviour?

BIBLE NOTES

Here Paul touches on some issues which are particularly sensitive in modern Western culture. We must note that here he makes only the briefest of targeted comments, presumably to address particular problems he had encountered in the church of his day. Contrary to the opinion of many today, Paul was not asking wives to be doormats, or to be scorned as inferior to men. He was being true to his conviction (3:11) that everyone is equal in God's sight. It's an echo of a passage from another letter: 'You are all sons of God through faith in Christ Jesus... There is neither... male or female, for you are all one in Christ Jesus.' (Galatians 3:26-28)

3:18-19 In Paul's day women were treated as possessions, creatures of a lower order, who were expected to do as they were told and were treated harshly if they stepped out of line. Paul's teaching challenges those attitudes.

The English word 'submit' has had many shades of meaning. The Greek word here is *hupotasso* (*hupo* 'under'; *tasso* 'in charge'). Paul is asking Christian wives to recognize the authority of the one who will ultimately be responsible to God for the family. He chooses this word in marked contrast to the word 'obey', which is his choice when referring to children (3:20) and slaves (3:22). Mary Evans, in her book *Woman in the Bible*, concludes 'nowhere in the New Testament is a wife exhorted to obey her husband.'

Jesus taught that no one should exalt himself (Luke 14:7-11), but that the greatest should serve the least (Luke 22:24-26). Paul's teaching asks wives to take on the role which God ordained, and in doing so he puts the husband in the role of head and therefore servant, to his wife and family. The picture is like that of a well-ordered regiment in which each person knows his role. All are of equal importance in carrying out the task assigned to them.

When Paul asks husbands to love their wives he uses the word *agape*, a term which is not used much outside the New Testament. It is quite different from the romantic love between a man and woman (*eros*); the love that exists between parent and child, or between friends (*phileos*), or the word which described the wish or desire for something (*thelos*). *Agape* is the word chosen when Jesus describes God's love for mankind; a love that caused him to give up his life for our sake. A wife is being asked to submit to her husband's *agape* love!

3:20 The word translated 'obey' can also mean 'listen carefully'.

3:24 Under Roman law a slave was not allowed to inherit anything. Paul speaks here of the total change made by Christianity. There is a reminder of the promise made by Jesus that 'the meek shall inherit the earth' (Matthew 5:5) and that those who do the will of God inherit 'the kingdom prepared for them since the creation of the world' (Matthew 25:34).

WORSHIP AND PRAYER

Pray for one another — for yourselves in your position within your immediate family and for others who live with you. If you live alone, or have no family, pray for those with whom you are in close contact.

Pray for the children in your local community: for those without Christian parents, for any you know who may be discouraged, and for those who are part of the church.

Pray, if appropriate, for your own work, for colleagues and for those who are directly in authority over you. Pray for specific local employers or for those in your church who are employers. Pray for any you know who are unemployed and seeking work, that they may not be discouraged.

>> See Sunday Extra on page 39 for ideas for songs and hymns.

Group Sheet

7

Growing Together

COLOSSIANS 4:2-18

AIM
To recognize the part we play in building up the church and in reaching others.

BEGIN HERE:
In groups of two or three, try to work out roughly how much of a normal day you spend in various forms of communication. How much time do you spend writing, reading, chatting to friends, talking to children, in discussion, on the telephone, listening to the radio, watching television? Now ask yourself how much of all your 'communication time' has a bearing on building up the church or drawing others to Jesus? Use your findings as a basis for discussion.

BIBLE STUDY
READ COLOSSIANS 4:2-18

Introduction
Our everyday conversation often reveals the things which concern us most. This closing section of Colossians is rather like that. It consists of a whole variety of instructions and greetings. As you read it you can pick up Paul's enthusiasm for sharing the gospel and for the growth to maturity of the church at Colossae. He writes of three positive ways in which Christians can be involved in this process.

KEEP IN TOUCH. First he asks them to be faithful and constant in prayer (4:2). This is an important part of our work for God. Without it we are unlikely to succeed. Paul particularly encourages the Colossians to pray for him as he proclaims the message about Jesus (4:3).
>> Now look at Question 1.

KEEP A LOOK-OUT. He then encourages them to seek opportunities to proclaim the message to those who are not part of the church. He urges them to speak in such a way that attracts people to Jesus, and to make sure that the way they behave endorses what they say (4:4-6).
>> Now look at Question 2.

KEEP GOING. Paul ends his letter with messages of encouragement and greeting for special friends within the family of God. He mentions:

the trustworthy — **Tychicus** *and* **Onesimus** *(4:7-9) who had worked closely with him to promote the cause of the gospel and whose job was to deliver Paul's letter to Colossae and to encourage the church there with first-hand news; by doing so they would demonstrate how the family of God links together, to uphold and sustain one another in the work of the gospel;*

the loyal — **Aristarchus**, **Mark** *and* **Jesus Justus** *who had worked and travelled with him, encouraging and supporting him in his final imprisonment;*

the prayerful — **Epaphras**, *already mentioned at the beginning of the letter, whom Paul knew to be a man with real concern for the Christians in Colossae;*

the obedient — **Luke**, *a Greek and a skilful doctor, had given all to God by joining Paul in his travels and staying with him to the end.*
>> Now look at Question 3.

Paul also mentions:
the disobedient — **Demas**, *who was later drawn away by the lure of riches (2 Timothy 4:10), which underlines the point that Paul made earlier, that the choice to follow Jesus is a continuing one: it must be backed up by daily deliberate choice;*

the givers — **Nympha** *and* **Archippus** *who were bearing the cost of discipleship. Nympha was risking much by having the church meet in her house, and Paul encourages Archippus, a leader in the church at Colossae (Philemon 2), to continue his work.*
>> Now look at Question 4.

Questions

1. How can we work at our prayer life? Together make a list of different ways in which you might review and enrich your private life with God. For example: a retreat, writing a journal, walking in the country. From the list each pick out one thing which you have found helpful in the past, and one you would like to try either again or for the first time.

2. How can you look and pray for opportunities to share your faith? How important is it to practise what you preach or should you only preach what you practise? Spend a few minutes discussing this. Each person could think of recent incidents when the way you have spoken or behaved has not backed up what you say you believe. Think of one way in which you might seek to change.

3. In what ways are you part of a team? Write down the names of three people whom you look on as fellow workers in the gospel. Look again at verses 7-9 and then describe those whose names you have written down in similar terms. Could you use what you have written to encourage them? If so, make a point of doing it in the next week.

4. How have you found discipleship costly? Spend a few minutes making a list. How can we counter temptation when, like Demas, we are drawn away from God's purposes? Discuss the two things that most easily blow you off course. Discuss a plan of action to help when tempted.

ACTION

Make two columns on a sheet of paper small enough to keep in your Bible. In the left hand column write the names of the members of your group. In the other column write beside each name the outstanding quality that you see in that person. Take each person in the group in turn and share some of the things you value in him or her. Keep the sheet and use it in your personal prayers, thanking God and praying for each one in turn.

Either individually or as a group, read the whole letter in one sitting, possibly in a version you have not yet tried (for example, the J B Phillips translation, or the Living Bible paraphrase). Move immediately into a time of prayer.

Growing Together

ALTERNATIVE METHOD OF STUDY

For this final study the alternative method is to look for the **Key Words** in the passage. Ask each member of the group to look for three or four key words or short phrases which highlight the main concerns of the passage. Then compile a list of your findings, allowing for some explanation of how these words sum up the passage. (This works best when everybody is using the same translation.)

ADDITIONAL QUESTIONS

1. Why do you think prayer is so important to Paul? How can we share his concern for prayer in the proclamation of the gospel? Would it be possible, for instance, to pray regularly in threes for three people each of you knows (the 'prayer-triplet' scheme)? Are there other ways in which you could pray?

2. Is preaching the gospel a job just for the gifted like Paul? How can each of us be involved in sharing the good news of Christ? How do we use everyday opportunities?

3. This passage reflects Paul's concern that Christians in one place should support those in another. How can we be similarly encouraging to believers elsewhere?

4. What does it mean to be a 'fellow-worker' with others? Why did Paul not work alone? Why is it important that we see ourselves as part of a team in the life of the church?

5. What else do you know about some of the people mentioned here, such as Mark, Luke and Demas? What lessons can you draw from their stories?

6. What indications are there in this passage of the cost of following Christ? What encouragements are there about the good things which result from following him?

BIBLE NOTES

4:2 Paul asks the Colossians to devote themselves to prayer. He asks them to be watchful and thankful; firstly so that their prayer-life avoids dullness and remains a vibrant conversation with God, and, secondly, so that they guard against slipping into the role of peevish children who will accept without thanks all that is given, and are always ready to ask for more.

4:3-5 He urges them to pray for his ministry of telling others about Jesus. He also shares with them two concerns for effective evangelism: firstly that God will create the opportunity for the gospel; secondly, that the message will be clear to those who hear it.

4:6 The word 'grace' is translated from the Greek word *charis*, which most often in the New Testament refers to God's love towards us. Here it has the more everyday meaning of attractiveness.

4:7-17 Paul ends the letter with personal messages from, and to, many of his friends. It is easy to assume that these are irrelevant and to skip over them. In fact they are integral to the letter. Taking a look at some of these people gives us insights into the family of God to which each of us belongs. In all the years of his ministry Paul had discovered the importance of belonging to that family; in nearly every letter he wrote, he names particular friends. There's much we can learn from studying the qualities of Paul's friends.

Aristarchus (4:10) was from Macedonia (Acts 19:29) and had stayed with Paul on his travels through Macedonia (Acts 20:4), to Jerusalem and on to Rome, experiencing the shipwreck and a winter in Malta on the way.

Mark (4:10) had gone with Paul and Barnabas on their first journey to Antioch and Cyprus, but had deserted them, causing Paul and Barnabas to argue and separate (Acts 15:38,39). Barnabas, however, encouraged Mark to put this initial failure behind him so that it did not blight the rest of his Christian life. He went on to work with Paul again and later to write his much-treasured Gospel.

4:16-18 Paul signs off in his own hand. He makes it clear that what he has written applies to more than the congregation at Colossae. He intends that they should pass his letters around and read them to the assembled churches. He reminds them that he is in prison on their behalf and prays for them to experience God's rich blessing, which rests on those who resolve to follow him.

 WORSHIP AND PRAYER
Meditate for a few minutes on David's prayer in Psalm 14: 'Set a guard over my mouth, O Lord; keep watch over the door of my lips'.

Each think of three things for which you want to thank God and then have a time of open thanksgiving, or join together in reading aloud Psalm 105:1-5a.

In a time of open prayer ask God to help each of you in the following areas: for growth in your own life of prayer; for willingness to seek opportunities to share the gospel; for the desire to speak and act in a way that draws others to Jesus; for the ability to work well with others in the church.
>> See Sunday Extra on page 39 for ideas for songs and hymns.

Sunday Extra

 No 1 Theme: Growing Together.
For an All-age Service you might consider building a shoe box wall, each box labelled with things and people in the church for which to give thanks. (Kneelers with labels might work just as well.) You could encourage members of the congregation to suggest thanksgivings. Include practical things (Mr X who does the church garden) but also give thanks for gifts of faith and love (Mrs Y for the love she shows to others) and for the ministries within the church. As the wall grows, make the point that it's people and their gifts, not buildings, which make the church.

Bring a good-sized pot plant to church. Talk about nurturing it so that it is 'bearing fruit and growing'. Point out the need for food, water, space, the right amount of light and the right temperature within the correct size of pot. Compare the needs of the pot plant to those of the church fellowship; emphasise the awareness we each need to have for one another, in order to encourage one another to grow.

For an adult sermon, set the scene for the coming studies by looking at the historical and cultural background to Colossians. Raid the Bible reference books for maps and diagrams. Share how the church at Colossae demonstrated each of the gifts of **faith**, **love** and **hope** which are the hallmarks of Christian growth.

Prayers for those who are engaged in pastoring and teaching, or in church planting would be appropriate. Suitable songs and hymns include the following found in Mission Praise:

30	Alleluia, alleluia	623	Take heart and praise our God
53	Because your love	631	Tell out my soul
88	Come bless the Lord	633	Thank you Jesus, thank you Jesus
104	Come to the waters	646	The greatest thing in all my life
113	Delight yourselves in the Lord	655	The Lord is a great and mighty King
151	For I'm building a people of power	701	Thou wilt keep him in perfect peace
560	Praise, my soul, the King of heaven	706	Thy loving-kindness
616	Stand up and bless the Lord your God		

 No 2 Theme: Developing and nurturing our relationship with God.
In this week's sermon you could concentrate on the Christian growth seen in:
1. Knowing God's will — and doing it (1:9-10a);
2. Knowing God's presence — and being set free by it (1:10b-14).

Alternatively look at what verses 15-20 say about Christ's relationship 1. To the Father; 2. To the world; 3. To the Church.

For an All-age activity you could ask some parents, as they come into the service, to write down answers to questions about the likes and dislikes (favourite meal, TV programme, pop group) of one of their children. During the service put the questions to the children and compare the answers! Make the connection that we need to spend time with God in order to know him and to discover how he wants us to live our lives.

Prayers might be for those whose task it is to teach the faith: youth and children's leaders, teachers, particularly those who teach in church schools, writers of daily study notes, ministers in your area. Ask especially that all of them may be given the gifts of wisdom and understanding.

Suitable songs in Mission Praise include:

6	Ah Lord God	339	In the name of Jesus
8	All earth was dark	361	Jesus, how lovely you are
14	All heaven declares	367	Jesus is Lord
30	Alleluia, alleluia	486	Now thank we all our God
38	As we are gathered, Jesus is here	624	Take my life
41	At the name of Jesus	625	Take time to be holy
139	Father, we adore you	735	We rest on thee

No 3 Theme: Being sure of our faith so that we can witness to others.
At an All-age Service you could interview one or two people, asking how they came to faith and what Jesus means to them. Focus on the convictions that underpin their Christian experience. For the talk, use a series of pictures of someone growing up — from new-born baby to adult. Talk about the growth Christians need to experience, from new birth to Christian maturity, relating this to Paul's concern for the Christians in Colossae.

An idea for an adult sermon would be to follow up the theme 'this is the gospel that you heard and that has been proclaimed' (1:23) and to talk about Paul's 'call' to witness, covering the following topics:
* **C**onfidence in Jesus and the message of the gospel
* **A**ssurance of forgiveness — for self and others
* **L**ordship of Christ — under his authority to speak
* **L**ove for others — wanting them to hear.

An idea for intercessions is to follow the 'finger prayers' exercise:
* **The thumb** is closest to you. Pray for yourself, and for a strong faith.
* **The index finger** points to others. Pray for those to whom you will witness: at home, at work, in school and in your local community.
* **The middle finger** is the largest. Pray for the world and all those who need to depend on God for help.
* **The ring finger** depicts covenant relationships. Pray for the Church throughout the world.
* **The little finger** is the smallest. Pray for those on the margin of your community who may feel lonely or isolated.

Appropriate songs and hymns include the following found in Mission Praise:

1	A new commandment	264	I believe in Jesus
73	Christ is made the sure foundation	266	I cannot tell
77	Christ triumphant	336	In my need Jesus found me
115	Do not be afraid	339	In the name of Jesus
142	Father, we love you	380	Jesus, stand among us
149	For God so loved the world	441	Lord of our life
151	For I'm building a people	541	One shall tell another
155	For this purpose		

No 4 Theme: the freedom we have in Jesus.

The sermon could be about

1. The fullness of God in Christ — the identity and saving work of Jesus

2. The fullness of life in Christ — how Christ sets us free.

Alternatively the sermon could teach about the service of baptism and its symbolism of the new life that we receive when we become Christians. A challenge to faith could be made and the renewal of baptism vows might be appropriate.

For All-age worship focus on verse 17 and talk about how a shadow is the related, but incomplete, image of a real thing. Place some familiar objects on the flat glass plate of the overhead projector so that their silhouette shapes appear on the screen or wall. You can get the same effect using a table-lamp with a strong beam. Compare the reality with the shadows. Go on to talk about how Jesus is the one who gives us real life. Sadly people allow many other things to rule their lives: not only alcohol and drugs, but also dependence on cult religions or occult practices including the reading of horoscopes. Things which seem to promise release from problems betray those who trust in them, causing them to live in fear instead of the freedom of love which God intends. Songs for worship could be chosen from the following list found in Mission Praise:

37 As the deer pants for the water	428 Lord for the years
254 I am a new creation	463 May the mind of Christ
331 In heavenly love abiding	488 O Breath of life
381 Jesus, stand among us	695 Thou art the way
382 Jesus take me as I am	715 Victory is on our lips
388 Jesus, we enthrone you	720 We believe in God the Father

No 5 Theme: Jesus sets us free from the past.

For a Family Service prepare two drawings, one of someone in old clothes and another of someone in brand-new clothes (or use real people!). Ask for suggestions about things which belong to the way of life of those who do not know Christ and label the person with old clothes. Then ask for suggestions about the things which should be seen in the life of someone who belongs to Jesus and label the other person. Link this to Paul's picture in Colossians and explain how Christ has made it possible for our lives to be changed. (You could also mention the practice, common in the early church, of the symbolic putting on of a new white robe when a new believer was baptised.)

For the sermon at an adult service talk about:

1. The principles of new life (3:1-4);　　　2. The practice of new life (3:9-17).

Prayers for deliverance from all that is evil could be adapted, as appropriate, from the Litany (Alternative Service Book, page 99). Appropriate songs and hymns from Mission Praise include:

21 All the riches of his grace	200 Great is thy faithfulness
26 All you that pass by	254 I am a new creation
33 And can it be	264 I believe in Jesus
57 Bless the Lord, O my soul	270 I get so excited, Lord
94 Come let us sing of a wonderful love	271 I give you all the honour
104 Come to the waters	435 Lord Jesus Christ

No 6 Theme: Relationships in the home.

At a time when many partnerships are under pressure, this could be an opportunity to preach on the marriage relationship. Sensitivity would be needed for the divorced, separated and single people in the congregation.

The service could include an exposition of the beginning of the Marriage Service (Alternative Service Book, page 288) and teaching on the marriage vows. You might like to focus on Paul's description of the family with its picture of the interdependent relationships between father, mother and children. Opportunity for the renewal of marriage vows might be appropriate.

For an All-age service show pictures of situations where there is someone in charge: a school, an aeroplane, a football match. Ask, 'Who's in charge here? Why is it important for someone to be in charge? Who gives them their authority?' Establish that ultimately we are all answerable to God. Then show pictures of a home and the members of a family. Talk about Paul's words in Colossians and how they help us to have a happy family life. You could also use pictures of the workplace and apply Paul's words about slaves and masters to that situation.

If your church would find it acceptable (and seating arrangements allow) prayer could be organized in small groups of six or eight. Alternatively you could use prayers adapted from the Marriage Service (Alternative Service Book, pages 298-300). Appropriate songs and hymns include the following found in Mission Praise:

1	A new commandment	133	Father, I place into your hands
25	All to Jesus I surrender	146	Fill thou my life
28	Almighty God, our heavenly Father	163	From the rising of the sun
32	An army of ordinary people	165	Give me a heart
69	Change my heart, O God	215	He has showed you
82	Cleanse me from my sin, Lord	232	His hands were pierced

No 7 Theme: Working together in the church.

In the sermon, focus on Paul's triple encouragement to Colossian Christians:
1. **Pray** — the need to pray for each other and for our witness;
2. **Preach** — the witness of evangelists like Paul but also of ordinary Christians;
3. **Promote** — Paul's desire to see others grow in their faith and ministry.

In All-age worship, use verses 4-6 as the reading. Talk about Epaphras. He had preached the gospel to the Colossians and continued working for them, from a distance, by praying.

Alternatively you could build up a visual aid of a group-photo of Paul's 'team' — all the people mentioned here. Describe something of their mixed backgrounds. Though all very different, all were able to share in Paul's work for the gospel. Make the connection with your own congregation today, stressing the need to work as a team to encourage one another and to share the good news of Christ. You could interview one or two people about the way they value the support of others in the church.

Pray for the preaching of the gospel and the life of the church (including its prayer-life!). Appropriate songs and hymns include the following found in Mission Praise:

129	Father God, I love you	578	Revive thy work, O Lord
218	He is here, he is here	624	Take my life
244	How good is the God we adore	630	Tell my people I love them
411	Let there be love	631	Tell out, my soul
412	Let's just praise the Lord	728	We have a gospel to proclaim

CPAS is an Anglican mission agency helping churches to evangelise, teach and pastor. Our staff work across Great Britain and Ireland to bring our fourfold mission of support to the local church and its leaders.

EVANGELISM

We help church members, both ordained and lay, to become more effective in their individual and corporate Christian witness. We offer a complete service for local church needs, from parish assessment work to preparations for missions, from adult training in personal evangelism to training in children's evangelism, from mission strategy for the local church to reaching the unchurched. Training is tailored to the practical needs and realities of the community in which the church lives.

LOCAL CHURCH LEADERSHIP

We help clergy and laity in their leadership roles. We do this by running training courses on a wide range of topics and by providing help and advice about specific parish situations. We publish an extensive catalogue of resources to help local church leaders and regular mailings tailored to the need of clergy *(Church Leadership Pack)*, Readers and youth and children's leaders *(CYFA Leaders' Newspaper, Pathfinder Pack and Children in Churches)*. We have a special programme, called Ministry Among Women, to help women discover their potential as leaders and to resource them in that role.

We nominate incumbents to over 500 parishes, making us the largest Patron in the Church of England after the Crown, and we make substantial grants each year to help churches pay for additional people to work with existing church leaders, especially in inner city areas. Our Vocation and Ministry Division run *You & the Ministry* weekends for those contemplating full time ministry. *CPAS Readers* gives the opportunity for meeting and learning with other Readers and finding out what other churches are doing, through conferences and publications.

YOUNG PEOPLE, CHILDREN AND FAMILIES

We provide biblical teaching, resources and training for the leaders of CYPECS groups *(CYFA, Pathfinders, Explorers, Climbers and Scramblers)* for young people and children in local churches. Each year over 10,000 children, young people and leaders attend camps and houseparties. Our *Ministry Among Women* unit also supports work among *Families and Under Fives*, helping churches to reach out into their communities in service and evangelism.

PUBLICATIONS

We are a major publisher of Christian resource materials, from workbooks to major video-based training courses for local church use on important themes of Christian ministry such as Christian discipleship and marriage. All our publications are subsidized to help churches afford them. Increasingly non-Anglican as well as Anglican churches and individuals are using our publications.

THE FUTURE OF CPAS

Our vision is to develop increasingly as a quality mission agency for the building up of local church ministry. We affirm the supremacy of Scripture in all our work. We are funded almost entirely by voluntary donations from individual supporters and churches.